ORANGE

VOLUME II: EVEN MORE LEFTIST STUPIDITY

Tarl Warwick
2023

COPYRIGHT AND DISCLAIMER

FOREWORD

After the thrilling success which was my first volume of short stories dealing with liberals and neoconservatives having various depraved encounters with Donald Trump, exposing the degenerated and often masochistic nature of their obsessions with him, I quickly decided that a second volume of lore was needed. There are so many people in the world obsessed with Trumps' genitals, his excrement, and which wallow in their delusions like pigs wallowing in a pile of their own urine-soaked feces.

The stories you are about to encounter are purely asinine and disturbed- as with the first volume of stories I released, none of the people here are based on real life figures- they're totally fictional, and any resemblance to real people is a coincidence. We will examine some severely disturbing things in this work; and I wish they were hyperbole- the product of my sick and twisted mind- but they are hardly that hyperbolic, and are based on some of the bizarre fantasies that TDS sufferers seem to harbor- a mental disease involving projection, self-hate, and morbid obsession. Trump tries to be helpful to these people; after all, he wants others to be happy and fulfilled. In their madness, a conscious admission of their passion for Big Don is rarely forthcoming.

Sit back a spell and enjoy this monumental work; one of the greatest political satire sagas ever to unfold...

ORANGE MAN BIG! VOLUME II

DEEDEES STORY

Deedee was a rock star, Deedee was angry.

Donald Trump kept using his music at his rallies. He had tried everything; publicly calling him a sick SOB, even going on news programs to rant about how orange man was bad. Deep inside he felt happy that his long-outdated music was being heard by more people than ever came to his increasingly sporadic concerts, but he was pissed anyways; how dare someone use his music without his explicit consent?

So he hatched a cunning plan- Deedee would go to the very next Trump rally, and confront Donald in person. And so, he did, while squelching his ass tight against his adult diapers, mindful that he had eaten a bit too much of the cheap, MSG laden noodles from the local Chinese food dive the night before.

He still had a lot of cash so he arrived in a limo, with a couple of groupies. Groupies were fun. In the past they threw their panties on stage at him. Now they usually threw their dentures. He didn't mind this a bit- the foul cheesiness in between the fake teeth was mighty tasty. Ozzy bit the heads off bats, and he made out with the dentures, so it was all good.

The big orange goofball was already on stage and Deedees song was already playing, so he made his way through the crowd, shouting and waving his hands, clambering towards the podium, mindful to try and not break his hip in the process. Trump saw him- gazed right through him- smiled, and addressed him. "Oh we got a rock star here folks, we're gonna party now, watch this Deedee, I know it's you. I can tell from the denture smell." The song ended and was replaced by a distorted tune similar to the prior- and a forklift wheeled onto the stage as Deedee stood in awe; on the end of the forklift was a human effigy, which Donald proceeded to shove his hands into, whirling them around in the likely *papier mache* human semblance.

"Oh yeah you're gonna take it, yeah baby shake it! Or however it goes." Trump danced side to side as he fisted the effigy, pulling out piles of hamburgers. "Only the best food for true MAGA fans!" Donald shouted and began tossing the burgers into the audience. The bloated mannequin was nothing more than pile upon pile of steaming hamburgers, and several staff began tossing mountains of french fries to the crowd from butterfly nets laden with grease.

Deedee was outraged- what a farce! A stray burger smacked him in the face and ketchup stained his eyes like cheap 80s eyeliner. "You got a spot on there!" said Donald, laughing. Deedee knew that this burger had been touched by the hands of Big Don himself. He couldn't take it any longer, falling to his knees and moaning, he sopped the burger along his face screaming about his sins, begging for forgiveness as he crammed chunks of meat into his pants, rubbing them on his shriveled half-erection.

"It's all good, Deedee, I wrote a book once. Best book ever. Never even mentioned hamburgers in it. I think that was a bad idea, wish I had a better copy editor."

Deedee writhed on the ground, covered in burger grease and stray french fries. He was so confused, so aroused, and so happy- he grabbed a MAGA hat that he found on the grease-soaked grass and cried tears of joy as he filled his pants with half digested MSG noodles, savoring the warmth and aroma, as the crowd tried to avoid the maniac, Donald laughing and laughing as Deedee fell deeper into hallucinations and delusions, passing out only to wake up back at home, with a complimentary burger tray already delivered, next to his bed.

OLIVERS STORY

Oliver squinted his untrustworthy eyes as he beheld the candidates before him; three thick hamburgers, supplied for his lustful, sordid depravity- he had been fornicating with hamburgers for years- it gave him a thrill, breaking that taboo- he was after all having intercourse with dead flesh, and it was therefore necrophilia, but it was also from a cow, and so it was a sort of bestiality. The hamburgers were carefully scrutinized- he was a bit choosy when it came to dating. He couldn't be choosy with human females, which he secretly despised, but hamburgers couldn't talk back. He wished he could work that concept into some of his news reporting but thought better of it; that would mean he would be swiftly unemployed and it's hard to buy hamburgers when you're poor.

He sighed. None of the three candidates were especially attractive; he'd have to pick the lesser of all evils to slide his tiny prick inside of. One was a bit greasy for his taste, another a bit thin- even a small prick needed a bit of meat-width to actually gain penetration- and the third was accidentally included- a soy burger- he wasn't interested in sex with plants as much as with animals, although he did screw a cucumber once. The seeds went into his urethra and hurt when he ejaculated them back out. This was not a fetish for Oliver.

Sighing again, he was about to unzip his pants, mindful to turn the several cameras in his newsroom off beforehand (not that he minded exhibitionism, he just wanted to stay employed.) Of a sudden, there was a buzzing on his desk; something had arrived for him.

"What is it?" He said, panting a little from the expectation of a half-assed orgasm.

"It's from... him." The voice said through his intercom, in a monotone.

"Salvation?" Thought Oliver to himself. "Bring it in!"

The package smelled like freshly charred flesh. His little peepee immediately pricked up. After his staffer left he read the little note pinned to the side- it gave instructions to call a certain phone number before opening the box he had just been handed. He did, and the call immediately went to voicemail.

"Oliver old buddy, I know you have trouble finding a date, but I have the best women. Really, beauties. I put on pageants and fashion shows Oliver, you wouldn't believe some of the gals there. Thought you might be hungry, so I sent you a gift. I owned a casino once. Bye."

Inside of the box was a big, beefy, perfect hamburger. This hunka meltin' love was his first true ten out of ten. He unzipped his pants faster than Mike Tyson at a speedbag, and slit a little opening before plunging his small wiener into the beef- it was the perfect temperature too, warm- it felt godly... That is, for the first ten seconds.

He withdrew his wiener, clutching it with both hands- the heat! The beef drippings seared into his urethra, burning with the heat of a volcano. He dropped to his knees, eyes tearing up. His phone rang and he managed to grab it without scattering everything on his desk, one hand on his crotch, the other answering the phone.

"This is an automated message" the caller said. "I thought I would spice up your sex life a little bit Oliver, so I had my chef fill the patty with pure ghost pepper mash. Don't worry, we removed the seeds first, I remember you mentioning your cucumber incident. My urethra never had any problems. It's a presidential penis, you know, gotta be healthy for America, I tried hard to avoid STDs Oliver, that was my own personal Vietnam. Hope you enjoy your very hot date."

The automatic message ended, but Olivers happiness had just begun. Big Don had finally done it- out-Heroded Herod, and had given him the ultimate divine experience. The pain, the punishment, for his depravity, sent waves of orgasmic ecstasy all up and down his spine. He slopped some of the ghost pepper mash out of the patty with his finger, and plunged it straight into his eyes, literally pushing his finger behind the eyeballs, painting his very optic nerve, then stuck some up his butt. The pain was too intense to bear, and he had a seizure, wracked with spasms on the floor, kicking and jerking like a poorly programmed animatronic mannequin, or a marionette wielded by an orangutan on ketamine.

Yes, at last, the final fulfillment of the greatest pleasure he had ever known. The pain lasted, and lasted, as he lay exhausted on the floor. In one final act of spiritual decrepitude, he consumed the burger, eyes watering anew through the spicy pain, consuming his lover, consuming her beefy flesh. He wanted to tell all the nation about what Donald had done for him, but he could not; and though he was happy, he harbored a secret fantasy about streaming the next such act live. He prayed to the confused god that created him in all his wretchedness, that Trump would send him *just one more burger* and vowed that he would if the opportunity came.

MARIANNES STORY

Marianne had ended her presidential run; it just wasn't panning out. Her message of socialism and meditating to stop wars didn't resonate with voters as much as it did in her wicca coven, and she was kaput; the embezzled campaign funds she had managed to launder through several third party entities was, in the end, only enough to buy out a decent commercial property on main street- but at least it was a living. She sold crystals, wands, incense, orgonite chunks, and most importantly, her sexual services, which were in the intermediate range as far as price went. The little alley behind the store stunk of fish and shame.

She wanted more, much more, in life. Sighing, as she organized and reorganized the amethyst specimens on the front counter; Salem was boring in the off season. Only two people had come in so far today- a drunken hobo who she ushered out, and a crazy-looking wiccan chick who milled around for an hour and left with a kombucha, muttering to herself about her headspace feeling odd.

A noise from outside drew her attention- a vehicle screeched to a halt, a ponderous slamming of a car door, and then heavy thudding footsteps. Worried about thieves, she was reminded that she had no weapon to defend herself, as she thought self defense would lower her karma. She rapidly lubed herself up just in case, prepared to sacrifice her dignity for the sake of reincarnating as something better, like a space alien, an indigo child with an actual political future, or perhaps a sea snake, as sea snakes rule.

The door fairly flew open and there he was; it was really him, the big orange fascist himself, Donald had arrived. Marianne stood silent and motionless as he slowly toured the front of the room, his agents standing just outside, leering in the door and watching her through aviator sunglasses, evil weapons of war on their hips.

"Nice place, Mary, or Merlot, whatever the hell it is." Trump swaggered down the middle of the store as he spoke, "I like some of these. Have several in fact" he pointed to some geodes. "I prefer my balls unbroken though." He chuckled at his own joke. Marianne could feel herself lubricating for the first time in twenty years. The lube she had applied to both holes was now superfluous. "Now, Marianne, I know you have a money problem. Here's ten thousand. I'll buy the geodes, you overpriced hoodwinker you. Maybe I can give them to cancer kids, maybe I'll toss them off the highway overpass during rush hour as a joke, you never know, right? Can't make a breakfast taco without cracking a few eggs right?"

He winked at her and scribbled on a check. "I expect the geodes to be packed up tomorrow, I'll have my friend Mike come and get them, he still owes me for the whole chastity belt incident. Weird guy, looks like George Bush somewhat, can't miss him. Well, take care."

Trump left as quickly as he came, grabbing a soda from the cooler in the front without paying for it, tossing the check to her as the door closed. He had saved her livelihood, that was clear. He had also made her side job much easier. She took five sausages in the alley that afternoon, and they slid in effortlessly. She was juiced up for days thinking about the encounter, and soon the geodes were shipped out- she even slimed one up real good so Donald could be reminded of her delicious hippie grandma scent. She hoped he would enjoy it and harbor as many fantasies about her as she did him.

STEPHENS STORY

Stephen was having some issues with his work- the ideas just didn't flow to him like they had in the past- indeed, he spent about half of his time on the internet looking for things to be irate at, and lashing out at people who were more important in the contemporary sense; he was stuck thinking it was the mid 1980s, and that his material was still "hip."

He furrowed his brow and stared myopically at the papers before him- nothing made sense anymore. A story about a dwarf that does drugs and kills people? That's a great idea, but he couldn't create a sensible plotline. What about a story involving a potato that comes to life and is capable of talking, trying to convince scientists to engineer it a cyborg body to interact with the world? He was stuck on page thirty, around the time the potato started to sprout out and was engaged in a psychological game of chess with the scientists, who were hesitant to help it, thinking it must be evil. He considered adding a section where a struggling, psychotic author shoves the potato in his ass and the potato likes it. He felt his publisher might look askance to the concept.

Many such cases. He jerked his half erect willy a bit under the mahogany table in front of him and sighed- it was a hot day, his balls dangled low and he had to make sure not to sit on them accidentally.

Just then, his office door opened, and a tall, handsome man swaggered through it, gesturing to some other people outside to wait. How he had entered his home was beyond Stephen, who stared, his tiny, beady eyes glaring at this apparent intruder; but they opened wide in just a few seconds, for there he was- Big Don. The orange orangutan had decided to pay him a visit, no doubt bribing his under-paid guard at the door to let him and his entourage into the home.

"Oh you gotta be kidding me" Stephen muttered, as he grabbed for the weapon he did not own, since he spent a full half of his time on the internet arguing that everyone should be disarmed so people wouldn't meet a fate similar to those in most of his novels. "What the fuck do you want?"

"I want a second hamburger, but there's no restaurant near here with good ones, Stephen." Trump was gesturing randomly, his face a stoic semblance of disinterest, gazing on the surroundings, "nice table. Mahogany is expensive. I have a lot of it. Sometimes I wonder if it was even legally cut. You know, Stephen, I read one of your works once, something about a pandemic that almost ended the world. Reminded me of the China virus." He pronounced China as "Chy-na" and Stephens willy stood up like a lingam.

"Donald... why are you here?"

"Oh come on I'm here to give you some ideas. Write a dirty novel. To hell with this dwarf on drugs stuff, write one about a president who gets attacked by a rabid dog and guts it and commands his scientists to engineer the rabies into a weapon and then he bombs the globalists with it. It'd be yuge, a best seller perhaps. Stop fiddling with your peter and get to work, Stephen."

Trump tossed a hamburger onto the mahogany table and left without a further word. Stephen was flummoxed- he was right, Big Don was, that was a plot he could get behind, and in a tizzy, not wanting to disappoint his best friend, he immediately set to work. At around midnight he passed out at his desk, face-first on the hamburger, smearing its condiments on his sleeping face, seventy pages of a rough draft already completed, having wet dream after wet dream until his trousers were layered like a baclava- he had a preliminary title, too; "Orange Man Big!"

GERALDOS STORY

In the night air, his ridiculous mustache whirled about like windmill blades as he shook out his slacks, making his way across the Mar-a-lago lawn under the cover of darkness, seeking to avoid security; the secret service he could always get around by bribing, like people did JFK's detail so long ago, but the regular security he'd have to avoid. He twirled the mustache like snidely whiplash and found a few crumbs of roasted pork in the hairs- he ate them, waste not want not. He swaggered as he walked, pretending he was on the set of a cheesy eighties spy thriller.

It was about time to discover the true nature of the Mar-a-lago classified documents which had been covered up for so long, and he was a journalist, dammit. He threw a few punches at thin air, in case he needed to knock someone out.

Up and over the railing and past several windows he went, staring in to see what was going on. The first room was empty. The second room had a few rich people in it- probably friends of his- tipping wine and making small talk. The third room was the real deal- where all the classified stuff had been. His hip ached from climbing the railing. "They make railings a lot higher than they used to" he mused, mindless of his own age.

Jiggling the window open upon finding it unlocked, he tried to snake his way in like a ninja but ended up careening to the floor, spraining his forearm in the process. But pain was for losers, and he popped a couple painkillers, expecting it to wear off in an hour or so. There were still some scattered boxes in the room, and he intended to quietly search each one. One empty box in the corner would serve as a hiding spot if anyone should come in.

But he was immediately confused. As he examined the contents of the first box, and then the second, and even a third, all he found were pictures of... himself. Thousands and thousands of pictures- from magazines, newspapers, printed-out stuff from the internet. He was totally lost. Just then, the door clicked open and Geraldo catapulted himself into the empty box, waiting to see who it was.

The person in the doorway breathed heavily and chuckled. "I know you're there Geraldo, you naughty boy. Narcissism, that's what they call it. I know you have a collection of pictures of yourself but my collection is bigger. Took a week to compile it. I'll just ignore your trespassing, even pay for your nights' stay myself. Have a good time and clean up when you're done. I own five golf courses, Geraldo."

The door clicked shut again and locked. He knew what Big Don had done for him. Tens of thousands of pictures of himself; some he forgot existed. He sat there, slowly disrobing, on the floor, jerking himself madly, the painkillers giving him bouts of euphoria as he beat off until there was nothing left but narcissism and nostalgic psychological dismay. Mindful of Trumps command to clean up after himself, he sadly, mournfully, used the precious pictures of himself to clear away his puddles of jizzum, crying and weeping and using the tears to help remove the mess. He was a bad boy- a very bad boy. He stuffed one of the pictures up his ass in penance, as, in the wee hours of morning, he gathered as many as he could into a box, and prepared to leave through the window from which he entered, once again hitting the tiles on the way out, hastily gathering stray pictures back up.

Upon returning home with his precious trove- which would occupy his fantasies for weeks- he realized he had received a text message. Donald had one last treat for him; a picture of the room lit only by blacklight, showing the glowing stains of his sin on the floor, with pictures of himself scattered here and there. A fine trophy, he thought- a memory of one of the best days of his life.

BRIANS STORY

Brian had chuckled when he got up that fateful morning; he had spiked his brothers' wine cooler so that he would be too hung over to accompany him on his great expedition; this day, he wanted to be left alone to his perverted birdbrain deeds.

He had managed to con one of his globalist investor buddies into securing him a spot aboard Trumps yacht- it was a nice one; four levels and about the size of a decent ferry. The affair of the day would be pretty comfy- only a few people had been invited so the decks wouldn't be too crowded. He hoped to get some cozy time alone with his favorite politician. He had a folder stuffed with screenshots of all the times he had whined about the man, hoping to humiliate him so that he could feel the lustful connection of mutual self hate. He harbored fantasies about that- about making Big Don show some emotions towards him, after all, certainly after so many long years, the Don must feel some sort of sadomasochistic symbiosis, no?

The day was clear but that evening there were storm warnings; maybe the ship would have to ride it out all night. He was hoping to be riding Donalds mushroom while lightning flashed through the portholes and the boat bucked up and down, thrusting that meat deep inside his intestines. He had made sure to take it easy on the wine coolers and heavy foods the last night and had taken an enema in the morning just to make sure he didn't accidentally poop on the presidential penis.

Donald, however, was not aboard when he arrived. He was confused. In fact, other than a few crew members there was nobody at all. The crew lifted the boarding ramp and began to shove off into the green waters, as he stood on the deck, wondering if he had been Shang-hai'd as a sexual servant or something. The idea certainly enthralled him. Every form of slavery was bad, unless it was Chinese twelve year olds making his next overpriced smartphone, or unless he was chained up in bondage gear in the brig aboard orange mans' personal vessel, waiting in masochistic impatience, throbbing in his masters' absence.

The captain handed him a letter, signed by the man himself. He couldn't help but lick the glue sealing it shut- he might have just absorbed some of Trumps' own tongue atoms. He was stiff as the mizzenmast. The letter was terse; "Hey Brian, I know you ditched your brother so I ditched the other guests so you could have privacy. Your room is in back. There's a surprise for you. Plenty of paper towels to clean up when you're done. I handed out paper towels to those poor people in Ohio there that time. Weird city government. Good people. I invest heavily in companies with good paper towels. Signed. Big D."

The room was large and the mahogany bed inside was a full on California King. Comfy, with satin curtains drawn around the portholes. In the middle of the room was a water tank containing a large, live fish, with a bow glued to its forehead. Brian was astounded- he had always been called fishfucker in school, and now by george thanks to Donald he was going to prove them all right. In a moment of pure ecstasy, he stuck his pole in the grotto and went fishing in the fish pond. Every moment was bliss. The fish must have been well trained, for it seemed to enjoy it. Also, his schooner was so small the fish may just not have noticed it enter the poop deck.

He passed out from pleasure and when he awoke the fish was no longer alive- silently, the crew seemed to have cooked it for him while he slumbered, and he ate every bit of that tasty flesh, grilled to perfection, served with mixed vegetables and a delicious lemony sauce. He said "grace" before touching a single bite though, almost worshiping Donald Trump before such a god-sent meal.

JOE STORY REDUX

Little Joey was having a bad day. He hadn't eaten his whole bran muffin and had been sent to take an early nap- and he didn't even get ice cream for being a good boy and not doodying his adult undergarments. Nervous secret service agents kept a close eye on the door, to make sure he didn't sneak out. He had tried to bribe them into bringing him just a little ice cream by promising to start a war but the ruse hadn't worked- they all knew it wasn't Joe calling the shots anyways and war declarations required a joint vote by the Trilateral Commission and the board of directors of several corporations.

He was miserable. Miserable, that is, until the phone rang. Everyone close to him knew it was not allowed by Jill to disturb his naptime, but he wasn't able to sleep anyways, because of his bad mood. He sneaked over to the phone and picked it up, answering in a hushed tone so as not to alert his guards. "Hey, can't talk right now, my wife will spank my poopy behind, fat, call back later."

"Don't hang up Joe, I have something that will cheer you up, it's in a little package just outside your window on a string, you should be able to haul it in. I invested in a lot of companies but never a string factory. Too risky an investment. Cats like to destroy string, lot of turnover. Anyways Joe, ciao."

The voice was awfully familiar. He managed to make it to the window without suffering a fall and cracked it slightly. The package was small and nondescript, with a note attached. It simply read "this isn't a bomb, the only bomb in the white house is the dirty one in Joes undies. D."

D must mean Donald! That old dog faced pony soldier was playing some sort of trick! Joe worried that it was a pile of glitter inside or perhaps some fart spray, but opened it anyways with a little pen knife he had smuggled into the mattress. His wife didn't like him using sharp objects.

Inside was a box, a cold box- a whole box of ice cream. On the box was a picture of Big Don himself smiling. It was a Neopolitan! It even had its own ice cream scoop on the side. Joe grinned like the hillbilly from Deliverance as he immediately dove in, savoring mouthful after mouthful of delicious ice cream. It was the best he had ever had.

The phone rang again and Donald was again on the line. "Oh Joe I forgot to mention, I know you didn't get enough bran today and that makes you get indigestion, so I spiked the ice cream with laxatives. Nothing too powerful, just enough to make you slide a hot loaf out of your asterisk asshole. Enjoy explaining that one to everyone!" He laughed and laughed before Joe put the phone down. He had indeed been tricked! Dastardly Donald!

Within minutes he could feel a tummy rumble, and the rumbling increased, wracking his intestines with turbulence. He had to go number two! He staggered to the door and begged the service agents to let him go use the potty, but they refused- they needed his wifes' permission and suspected he was trying to trick them so he could go play with his toys or do something naughty.

Heaving, he bent over double as one agent tried to get Joes' woman on the line, but before he could establish contact, Joey filled his presidential pants with a sickening slurry of half digested slop. The laxatives had pushed out everything- clumpy bolus, squishy yellow goo, and a tidal wave of rectal nectar, which poured down his slacks to the carpet below, which was no longer a stately blue but a morass of bowel movement, slushy and foul. The scent was too much and the agents backed away, shouting into their phones that they needed a hell of a cleanup on Pennsylvania Ave. But Joe was not done. He continued to heave out shit, taking off his pants as it sprayed wildly in all directions, before getting a bright idea- he turned around and fired a splattering blast of excrement at the agents which had dared defy his authority and prevent him from having ice cream- after all, Donald had certainly given it to him- and as the shitting subsided, his indigestion was clearing up. Trump was, it seemed, a healer and not just a warrior.

The agents fled, as his wife hurried around the corner to confront her misbehaving child of a husband. He smiled widely at her and she froze in her spot. She knew that look- he may be old as hell and decrepit but when he got "that" look in his eyes he was about to do something extra naughty. He turned on one foot, lowered his head, and grunted as he force-shat out the last bolus of solid poo in his asshole, with the force of a Howitzer launching a shell at an orphanage, burying children alive in rubble. The dribbling anal backwash fired it with great efficiency, and, splat! The bolus hit his wife square in the face, painting it like she was going to a minstrel show- he used to enjoy those back in the day. He laughed as hard as Trump had laughed- the old crook may have tricked him, but he had used that trick to great advantage- what a genius strategist!

After a short chase, his wife roaring and commanding him to be seized and put in time out, he was caught, and reprimanded by having to sit in his own poo before showertime. He grinned the entire time, half dazed by dementia, remembering Donald, that big oaf, who had accidentally enabled one of his most glorious moments. He relished the stench of his own innard slop as he sat there, knowing that the agents would have to spend days wading through his foulness, his exasperated wife drinking heavily to wash away the anguish of being so treated.

NEW YORK DADS STORY

The child support bill had come in. After years of being a deadbeat, finally the bell tolled for he, and there was no escaping it- he was in some deep financial shit. Sure, the DNC funding helped a lot, but it wasn't enough. He'd be paying through the nose for years to come, and his neoliberal masters were not willing to loosen their purse strings to give more cash to someone who could be paid a pittance to regurgitate their talking points- younger and much more popular figures would do it for the same price. In the end, he should be happy he was paid at all given his limited reach and poor reputation.

This sad dad, this Brooklyn crook, finally had no option. He dialed the one man he knew could set his books straight- and that man was Donald Trump. He only knew how to contact him after a brief business meeting years prior with some globalists and a handful of military complex mercs who frightened him enough for his bowels to release in his pants. They were serving exceptionally spicy curried veggies that day though so nobody noticed.

He rang the number, sweating profusely. If he didn't con the Don into paying his child support, he'd be up shit creek without a paddle or a boat- but the call immediately went to voice mail. "Hey daddy-O!" Trumps' recorded message drawled on the "O" excessively, and a guffaw or two issued from the recording thereafter. "Look, I know you have money issues. Everyone does. I was broke a couple times on paper, but I still own skyscrapers. Skyscrapers are useful, you know, they scrape the sky, then you clean them off and all that dust and soot runs into the gutter. My skyscrapers are very clean, and I figure this is environmentalism in action. We need more skyscrapers, especially ones with my name on them. I'll give you a small loan but I need something in return. Stay tuned."

The message ended with a beep. What did Big Don want? The sorry, crack addicted man slumped in his chair momentarily before a call came in. He picked it up and waited, breathlessly.

"To receive your one hundred thousand dollars, you must drop your trousers and wait at the window."

It clicked off again with a beep.

Obediently, the man dropped his pants and waddled with them still around his ankles to the window of his bedroom, wondering what shenanigans were afoot. Then, a drone swooped out of the sky, pelting his bum with pellets from a mounted pneumatic rifle. Oh how it made his sinful zone smart! Little red welts, some dripping blood, were cratering his ass cheeks like lumpy piles of swiss cheese as he bent over, crying and begging Donald for mercy. And the drone was mounted with a camera- a small speaker on the thing announced that the "video would be uploaded" and he'd "have his share of the loot."

One last shot hit him right in the cock, and he bent over, penis bleeding and ruined, grabbing his wretched crotch, but orgasming anyways, delighted in his masochistic frenzy. He had served his role, and knew Big Don would deliver more than just sexually.

The video of this incident went completely viral. A hundred million people saw it. In the end, his cut of the ad revenue alone was far more than he was promised- and with his child support paid off for the next decade, he worshiped Trump, depraved himself on the floor, humping his carpet, wishing only that he would send his drone back for round two. Like a cargo cultist worshiping a plane made entirely of bamboo, he spent days by the window, eyes glazed in fervor and determination, aiming every bit of his will on making it come back, so he could have one more such experience- an experience of pure bliss.

THE GREAT DNC INVASION

The big day had finally come. The DNC was gathering-and all of the usual suspects were there. Hippies, billionaires, con artists, and nepotistic delinquents. But there was one thing conspicuously missing; the catering service had been burned down the night before the convention because of a tragic accident involving a diversity hire janitor incapable of telling the difference between kerosene and window cleaner, and food was scarce. Everyone was starving. That is, until one hell of a delivery came through.

At about 9AM, two large commercial trucks pulled into the side bay outside of the convention center, with orders to unload their goods; the guards waved them through. By 10AM, the work was complete, and the crates were being opened and deliveries made to the kitchen.

There was food aplenty; burgers, hot dogs, platter after platter of salad, there was juice, and beer, and an enormous quantity of wine- probably enough to satiate Nancy Pelosi for an entire weeks' vacation. The hot wings were spicy. The deviled eggs were perfectly seasoned with paprika. The steaks were enormous and vacuum sealed in their own juices- but nobody knew who had shipped the food, only that the manifest was real, the food wasn't spoiled, and security had been told the delivery was coming, so there was nothing to complain about.

The first inaugural day of the convention itself was a boring affair- a dozen Democrats droned on stage for between fifteen minutes and a half hour apiece, as the audience clapped warmly, occasionally breaking out into wilder applause, normally when the person on stage mentioned that they wanted to ban the second amendment, imprison political dissidents, or start a war with some third world nation.

The Soviet affair continued into the afternoon before the crowd at large was ushered out so the politicians and their moneyed, elite allies could gorge themselves on the food which had been prepared in the convention halls' kitchen.

Attendees began to eat. It was sumptuous- nothing was lacking. But about fifteen minutes into the meal a booming voice was heard in the convention hall, which was now filled with tables covered from stem to stern in platters of food until the table legs bowed out from the weight. The voice was that of Donald Trump.

"Unions are a disaster, the union catering company you were using was bullshit. Trump steaks are the best steaks. We make great Greek salad too, the secret is caraway. I have a lot of it, lost count of the number of caraway packets we had to use. Anyways I spiked all the foods with libido enhancers so you're gonna have a great party tonight. Make sure to sober up before tomorrow... unbelievable."

Donald had indeed spiked all the food. The most gluttonous gourmands- led by Christie, who had sneaked in just for the free food and was welcome anyways because of his political ideology- were quickly aroused to the point of nymphomania. Even the pick-and-peck light eaters were feeling the rush, and all of the seeping depravity of usually elderly flesh came surging to the surface, sexual arousal practically dripping from their pores as an enormous orgy convened.

It was a hideous affair. Piles of aging, sagging flesh, clothes torn off, thousand dollar suits discarded like trash, sometimes in the food trays themselves, as drunks, druggies, and sex starved ancient sots cavorted together in a grand display of hedonism which would make Marquis DeSade blush. It was like a scene from a poorly made porn film, where a thousand humans simply heap together, humping anything that moves and sometimes inanimate objects, just like animals. Like a beach full of seals, flopping around with their juices freely flowing, fucking one another with utter abandon.

Liver spots and wrinkled, sagging breasts, withered, discolored scrotums, weak tricklings of ancient sperm from elderly penises, all mixing together, with the occasional generation Z attendee invited to make the party look less ancient attempting to find a mate within ten years of their own age. Everyone from former presidents down to those invited solely because they were not old and white, for the purposes of making the party seem more inclusive, were whacking off on one anothers' faces, and burying themselves in every hole. Every hole took multiple digits and several phalluses. Even some phalluses were mounted, as the dockers began to work their way through the orgiastic cavalcade of Mammon. It was fitting that the light was dim and largely wall-directed for their dinner- in the delusional minds of some attendees, it was like being in a temple dedicated to Moloch, and they were all acting like the beastly barbarians they were.

Thanks to Big Don, they had not starved, and as their aging libidos finally gave out, many attendees weren't even able to find the strength to return to their private rooms at the hotel next to the convention center, leaving hundreds of mostly naked or half-naked, drugged up, elderly perverts passed out on the floor. A few spectacularly gifted libertines even managed to pound down seconds, feasting some more, before holding their own private mini-orgy. Nobody was knocked up that night, but they were all impregnated with a reverence for the big man, who had given to them the gift they had all always wanted.

MADDOX' STORY

Maddox was a sad man. He had been relevant in political discourse for some time, but times had changed, and he was a relic, a shadow of his former self. He decided that it was time to end it all.

A ring at the door distracted him from repeatedly trying and failing to tie a noose to hang himself with. "Fuckin shit" he muttered, tossing his failures aside as he went to the front door. Outside there was nobody, just a package. Opening it, he found a small packet of cement and a note; it was terse.

"Hey Maddox" it went, "I know you wanna off yourself. Mix this cement with some banana flavored oatmeal then go for a swim. Sayonara, senor, or however it goes."

Drowning seemed like a decent way to go- the local press might run with the story, after all, it would obviously be a deliberate act, and the corporate media loved its sob stories. So he obeyed the note. He mixed the cement powder with oatmeal and milk. Boy, it tasted foul. He supposed the banana part was to mask some of the flavor. The cement lump in his stomach weighed him down like an anchor as he finished his last meal and launched himself into his small swimming pool one last time.

But it was not to be. As he felt himself drifting out of consciousness, flailing to surface but repeatedly being dragged down by the lump of cement hardening in his stomach, he felt a hand reach down, like Frodo pulling Samwise Gamgee out of the water and onto a boat and, sputtering, felt himself lifted onto the pool deck.

There he was, backlit by the sun like Jesus Christ himself, looking down on the sad, pathetic Maddox, having hauled him out of the water. He had a swimsuit on that said "Big 45" and was holding a bottle.

"Alrighty Mad bucks" he said, "now it's time for the chaser" and shoved the bottle of chalky liquid down Maddox' throat. "This'll clear you right up. Never use the stuff. My bowel movements are regular. Sorry but I just took one in your bathroom."

The liquid was a powerful purgative. Maddox vomited on the pool deck, working out clumps of cement, which had only partly hardened, spackled with caked clumps of oatmeal. Every bit of the cement came surging out like a waste slurry, until his guts were as empty as his wallet. He felt like a human dump truck.

"You know, back in the day they used to give people a purge to cheer them up. So cheer up Mardock!" Trump tossed him a pile of french fries, pirouetted around the edge of the pool deck in the semblance of a ballerina, and disappeared around the side of the house. Maddox was turned on- madly so. He grabbed a clump of his own cement vomit and rubbed it all over himself in a lascivious manner- he had lived another day, and now he had been justified by Donald himself. Maybe life wasn't so bad after all, maybe someone really cared about him- he tweaked his nipples thinking about this fatherly, familial love he had never experienced, and though the neighbors called the police in this crazy man playing with himself with clumps of vomit, he was ecstatic while in the drunk tank, answering all questions posed to him with nothing but jubilant laughter.

GRETAS STORY

Her autistic, scowling face was contorted slightly- Greta had smelled something from the kitchen, and it didn't smell vegan. "How dare you!" she cried out, pounding her fists against her head and the wall in frustration. The cook, on her private yacht, very calmly explained that the oven was powered by a battery chalk full of Chinese lithium mined by slave children, and was not in any way using a fossil fuel- he apologized for the smell, and said simply that he had indigestion, nervously flipping the soy patties on the grill. Although Greta screwed up her face in a weird manner, she seemed satisfied, and turned around, to go above onto the deck, overly long hipster sweater practically trailing the ships' deck like a cloak. She turned around only long enough to admonish the cook to hold in his sin-gas or else the world would soon be uninhabitable.

A small boat approached her lavish yacht. It had nobody aboard, and buzzed in slowly, sidling up to the side of the deck, apparently controlled remotely. Her fears of it being loaded with explosives was, in the end, unfounded- it would be her crews' anuses exploding, not the boat itself.

Aboard, as its contents were hauled up, were a variety of foods- all of them vegan. There was crate containing nothing but packet after packet of curry masala, there were lentil dumplings, and all the other wonderful ethnic foods she loved to appropriate. Greta was on cloud nine- you could smell the curry through the packets. It was going to be a fun night.

The crew, comprised of a captain, a cook, and two hands, along with herself, dipped into the delicious stash almost immediately. The little boat had come equipped with a warming unit, so the food was able to be served immediately- she had tired of the cook aboard the ship, who tended to prepare only basic

European meals, and potatoes and cabbage were fine, but after a while, you crave something a bit more exotic.

The curried masala was spicy. The dumplings were decadent and perfectly steamed. There was a non-vegan yogurt concoction of some sort which the crew gorged on but Greta did not know if the cows producing the dairy product were free range, so she skipped it, although she did sample a bit of the *aloo palak*, a spinach-rich meal with paneer- a sort of unsalted, compacted cottage cheese.

The inevitable kicked in about two hours later. The ship only had one toilet, and it was occupied continuously by a rotating assortment of crew members for hours thereafter. Greta was driven into a mentally abnormal rage as she had to listen to four peoples' assholes squirt out poo and release splattering blasts of sin-gas. She was holding her own in, not wanting to be a hypocrite, but at long last, the toilet still occupied, she released her bowels, stinking up the entire ship as she dribbled excrement all over the poop deck. The little boat had been skimming around the ship in slow circles, like an aquatic moon orbiting a planet, and a small speaker on it was activated around the time she humiliated herself in front of the crew by shitting her own pants.

"Greta!" it said, "How dare you!"

The echoing voice of Donald Trump reverberated in her head and she fled to her cabin, locking the door, hunching down, smeared with her own feces. Big Don had given her the meal of her life, and now she crouched, on the floor, in her clutter-littered room, sobbing with joy and with humiliation- he had indeed known exactly what she wanted. Just to pass gas, one time, to sin, to deprecate her existence as the world slowly trudged towards its inevitable demise at the malevolent hand of mankind.

EMMANUEL STORY

Emmanuel was a sick man, but he had some good connections.

He liked to refer to himself as Nero, gazing out at the Parisian landscape as it burned, laughing slightly and mindlessly strumming a harp, but even more he liked two things; eclairs and far older women.

This time though the riots were a bit more formidable- and they involved a protected religious class in his nation which he could not directly defend against. It was a sad state of affairs. The streets of Paris were beginning to resemble a Libyan war zone- the irony of which amused, but also alarmed him, simultaneously.

In the soaring halls of his presidential retreat, he basked in luxury like the Kings of France had centuries prior, nibbling on snails and tippling wine- a life he had grown accustomed to, but his envoy interrupted him with an urgent message; he had been given a delivery by a major US political figure, the envoy related, and it smelled amazing.

"Sacre Bleu!" Emmanuel shouted, starting up from his fainting couch and stuffing his half erection back into his trousers as he waltzed to the door, to retrieve whatever delicious entrees had been sent to him. A short note was attached. "Emmanuel!" It read, "No hard feelings. We didn't always get along but then nobody does. Sometimes my wife gets mad at me for watching too many internet clips of gorillas fighting. It's an inside joke but she has never gotten it. I also fought with my vice president. Weird dude, looked like George Dubya, kind of acted like him too. These eclairs are from Trump Tower. We have the best eclairs, even better than the French make them. Moist and delicate. I think you can handle the rest."

Emmanuel nearly cried with joy- they did smell delicious. Nice and chocolatey, lots of eclair cream stuffed inside. He wanted to shove one on his dick immediately but figured he should share... so he summoned his elderly wife.

She splayed her mottled old legs out on the fainting couch and Emmanuel proceeded with his favorite act in the world- eclair intercourse. He slid the thing inside her ass, and proceeded to fuck the cream, chocolate oozing out of the orifice as he stammered out random French sentences, usually involving "*couchez avec*." The cream worked its way up into his urethra, and he briefly stopped to pee some of it out on a portrait of Donald Trump- oh what a man! He was into men too, normally those from foreign colonies which had once belonged to his great and storied nation, but he had never dared broach the subject with such a powerful leader who, after all, had subjugated his presidency entirely.

He never managed to finish off though, as the phone rang halfway through the sex session- it was a recorded message from the DNC telling him he needed to sober up and get with the program, or else their globalistic plans would fail. With blue balls, he retired from his efforts, his ancient wife at least satisfied- she would probably eat the eclair remnant later- and though he was sad he was not allowed to finish off inside the dessert, he had a dozen more of them for later, and he was going to screw every Trump Tower eclair one after the other, until their stale cream caked every surface in his presidential bedroom. The big man had delivered, and his thoughts dwelt in heaven for days as he unleashed his cream into the *crème.*

ANDY STORY

Donald had a short stop-over in a liberal community. In between rallies, as his airplane was refueled, there were some sporadic protests by those who disliked him. This, he did not mind- it happened even in places where he had major political support.

But he stopped up short as he waltzed around the airport, greeting some fans and grinning at hecklers. There was one hell of a bad smell coming from one of the lounges off to the side of the terminal- a sort of spa.

He decided to investigate, tidying his tie and waving in secret service ahead of him; the smell turned out to be an entire tub full of fish sauce, in which one very smelly, sweaty man was bathing, while slapping his own face, muttering to himself about universal basic income.

Andy was coated in a sheen of sweat. He was clearly trying to remove it, splashing fish sauce across his body, then scrubbing it with a sponge, but it wasn't helping- his copious sweaty pores leaked salty water all across his body, and he was in the throes of agony.

Eager to help this poor man, Donald approached, although holding a rag to his face to deal with the smell- a smell like a tidal pool full of dead, rotting fish, as a tyrannical sun blazes down, heating the water, making garum. "Andy my man" he said, looking solemn, "I am afraid your fish sauce won't work. Poor bastard, probably been doing this for years. I'll tell ya, at Trump Tower he have something better for excessive perspiration. Never had that problem myself, but you should see Jared when it's hot outside. Incredible."

He proffered two items to the tormented man, who continued to bathe in his salty dead fish brine and tread water. The basin he was in was like a small pool, stained brown with the fermented fish waste. He hadn't even left the spa pool for some time so there were some turd floaters scattered around like a little anal armada.

First he tossed Andy a wool sponge, and then fiddled in his pockets for a moment before producing a lump of rock salt. "Never go anywhere without rock salt Andy, I invest in some salt mining companies. Useful for situations like this. Very sad." Trump lumbered back out of the room, eager to get away from the scent, as Andy began to crush the rock salt and rub it on his body, working it into his pores with the wool sponge. The exfoliation was exuberant- the saltiness was swell. He reached down and began to scrub his genitals- which shone anew, free of their sweaty sheen. The superior quality salt began to operate on his pores- and he stuffed some salt in his asshole as well, then wiping it with the wool sponge, shouting about police brutality. Save for himself the spa was empty, so he took the opportunity to whack off his small peter. The whole time he was thinking about the magnificent man who had finally cured his grotesque perspiration problem. The big man himself, Big Don.

PETE STORY

Pete was rather sad, standing on the platform looking at some of the dilapidated trains slowly whistling through the station- why is it that the United States had such a poor and underdeveloped rail system? He knew the geography wasn't like that of Western Europe, but he felt a maddening jealousy all the same.

Over the intercom there came a familiar voice, it advised that a special train was pulling in to the station, and that Pete should head to the track itself. "It will be unbelievable" the voice told him "best day of your life."

Pete headed down to the track, wondering what the fuss was about. He was still in Dracula-esque doldrums at that moment, still depressed, but anticipating, perhaps, the reception of some foreign dignitary who would want to shake his hand and take a few photos. At least the day would be less boring.

Instead, around the bend beyond the station, a train slowly chugged along, approaching- it was an old school train, the kind that use coal and steam. Smoke billowed from its stack as it went "chug chug chug", each rotation of its steam engine firing spray from its compression system. It was moving at about ten miles an hour as it approached- the engine all red and freshly painted, like something you'd see on a postcard in the 1910s.

On the front of the engine was a prominence- a gigantic dildo. Pete realized what his mission was- he was about to run the ultimate train.

Thankfully he carried around some mineral oil with him wherever he went- just in case. He ripped his pants and OSHA goggles and helmet off and lubed up his asshole, as the train continued to chug along. This was going to be one for the ages. As the train grew closer, he could see that the conductor was none other than Big Don himself, who smiled and waved and shouted incoherent things about stanley steamers cleaning more than just carpets, as the engine slowed a bit more, approaching at a painfully low speed.

Pete obeyed his fate, bent down, holding his asshole open before the dildo-train, poised atop the track itself, awaiting his moment of full salvation, of complete gratification. It chugged towards him, dildo wiggling, and he hoped it would not slip to the side instead of *inside*, resulting in him being crushed by the steam engines' wheels. But it slid in effortlessly into his dripping, oil slacked anus. It shoved right up inside of him, snaking through his intestines, lifting him up off the track. Some sort of hydraulic was involved, for the dildo lifted itself up both vertically and horizontally, and he found himself hoisted into the air like he was being sodomized by a forklift.

"Hey Pete!" the conductor shouted, "I have the best train! I call it the big one, because it's big and beautiful, just like America! Just look at that steam compression. Coal is a good thing, we need to stop waging war on coal counties in Pennsylvania."

Pete was astonished. His final wish had been fulfilled. The train picked up speed and soon they were whizzing past the countryside. As he orgasmed uncontrollably he saw trees, and little towns, cities, plains, all the bounteous beauty that America had to offer.

Then he woke up, the acid having worn off. His fantasy had been almost as good as though it were real. With nectar trickling from his bunghole, he sobbed, wishing that Donald had given him the ride of his life, but he was left with only drug induced fantasies.

CHARLES STORY

King Charles was rather in a dour mood. His breakfast had been late, and was rather overcooked, so after berating the chef, he decided to take a very solemn, typically British stroll through the local copse and sit by the pond there, sulking. He didn't have much else to do this day, other than shake hands with a few dignitaries and pretend he didn't look down his starched suit at them.

The weather was also stereotypically British. A light wall of fine mist settled on his suit, dotting it with dew drops, which he had an attendant wipe away with a silk cloth. On a rock by the pond he sat, muttering about empires and other British topics.

Just then a bubbling in the pond erupted, about ten feet away from the stone where Charles sat. Attendant and guards alike perked up, as the big, powerful man himself rose from the depths, casting aside a scuba mask and tank, standing there, elevated out of the water by some strange force, cherubic and dressed in a white toga, with a crown of leaves on his head. Donald Trump had decided to pay Charles a visit.

"Donald! How, why? What's going on?" Sputtered the aging king, confused at the sight.

"Don't worry about it Charlie. I had them put a little platform under the water which is hydraulic. Hydraulics are great. You can use them to lift things. Paid about fifty thousand dollars for it. Fifty. Thousand. Those Belgians really do good hydraulic engineering. Sorry it isn't made in the United Kingdom." Trump was pirouetting on the platform, just above the water line, lifting his hands like a ballerina for effect, and doing a sort of silent interpretive dance. "This is what they call theater, I think" Donald mused.

Charles was getting horny, but he was also rather hungry. Since he hadn't eaten more than a few bites of his breakfast his stomach was beginning to growl like a bear after Morvidus. "Anyways Charles I have something for you, cooked right at Trump Tower in London an hour ago. I think you'll find it tasty."

The toga wearing Trump slowly disappeared back into the water after tossing a small sword up onto the grass beside King Charles, which he held, not knowing what it was for. A second attendant rushed over, with box, and orders to deliver it to him. Inside was a pie of some sort, and it smelled heavily of carrots and herbs and meat and all sorts of other good things. Charles used the sword to carve off a piece- eating it on the edge of the blade, because he lacked a fork or spoon.

It was a game pie! Trump knew what he liked- game pies were meant for one thing, and that was anal pleasure. He commanded his guards and attendant to bend over and drop trouser, and began stuffing chunks of meat and carrots and piles of slopping gravy into their rectums, and when they were full, he stood, hand over heart, gazing into the distance, and thinking of empires long since dead.

At his command, those assembled fired the gravy and meat out of their assholes like human cannons. One final resolute shot for the empire. One final blast into the face of turpitude and despondence. Charles cried. Trump really knew him by heart, and it filled him with joy that such a great leader would honor him. The day was not dour or sad, and the sun shone a bit through the failing mist, as he and his gravy-stained entourage returned to business. A glass or two of wine, with another slice of pie, and Charles was ready for a bit more work that day.

JEB STORY

Jeb was a rather hungry man. Unsold guacamole bowls lined the shelves of his DC office, but there wasn't a hint of guacamole around. Not a taco. Not a tamale. He was hard up, and he had also fallen off the wagon again- he felt time throbbing through his drunkenness, just a shot or two shy of the room spinning out of control.

The bowls themselves- some five hundred or so- were nothing more than painful reminders of his failure, which he reveled in, in his masochistic insanity. He fiddled with himself and shoved a small plastic turtle up his ass, hoping to dislodge a turtlehead and cream himself, but it was not to be. He sobbed in disgrace at the hollow shell he had become.

But his sadness was not to last. His door flew open just then, a strong gale of wind blowing bowls all over the place, clattering on the floor. It was him! Donald Trump swaggered through the door, a huge fan behind him in the hallway, blasting bowls, papers, and pens around on the floor and tables.

"Jeb! You sorry sack, you must be hungry. Gimme that bottle."

Trump did not wait to be handed the bottle of liquor, he simply grabbed it where it had fallen, emptied it in the trash can, and tossed the empty remnant to the side. "This stuff is no good, ruins your health. I never drank anything, other than soda. Soda is great. Contains caffeine. I sleep four hours a night."

Big Don produced a platter and set it down on the table. There, in the center, was the biggest goddamn slurry of guacamole Jeb had ever seen, ringed by a whole fringe of tamales- perhaps fifty of them- and a huge, crescent-shaped bowl of nacho chips. To top it all off, there was another platter on the other side of the tray, with a bowl of *menudo* and a couple of taco bowls filled with meat, cheese, and other goodies.

"I know you're drunk Jeb, your wife won't like that. You won't be able to grab her by the pussy if you can't even walk. No good. You need some wholesome food. Now get off this bender and go do a couple fundraisers or something."

Big Don left then, and Jeb was enthusiastic about his lunch- not really a lunch, more like a multi-day feast. He was glad he had a refrigerator in his office. Unlike his small, paltry, guac bowls, the Trump bowl was an enormous affair, probably held about a gallon of guac- he kissed it, caressed it, smearing tamale grease on his face, he began to gorge, and gorge, smashing taco, tamale, nacho, and guacamole, down his gullet, staining his suit and the table, working himself up into a sexual frenzy. He briefly considered going into competitive eating as he realized he had eaten almost half the tray, but all that booze was bubbling up around the food in his stomach. He felt vastly sick, puking up green slime into the office carpet. Immediately, he felt less drunk, and even more hungry, smashing down several more tamales, dipping them deep in the guacamole- which was perfect. Not too much garlic, just the right avocado consistency. He whipped out his wee wee and smooshed it into the bowl, and delusionally imagined that he was docking Donalds much larger penis, penetrating the urethra, feeling the garlic rub his small phallus, as he moaned ecstatically, crying in joy- his stomach issue was solved, and he promised to get back on the water wagon, for he now knew true joy, and no longer needed to self medicate with alcohol. Big Don had truly delivered. And although he would have to publicly denounce his hero, like Saint Peter claiming he did not know who Jesus was, he would secretly be voting for him at the ballot box.

KARINE STORY

Being the boss was good. It was good to be sassy. You may not win many friends, only people scared to disagree, but you get paid a lot, and there's something satisfying about being able to simply glare at a member of the secret service and they bring you a coffee.

That's how Karines' day always began and ended, smacking down the misogynists left and right. But she felt somehow empty- something was lacking woefully. She wanted a powerful man to charm her handily, and there were no strong males anywhere in D.C. Most of them could barely hobble around, and the rest were soy sucking dipshits.

So, in her office, she held her head up high, while secretly wishing someone would actually be able to command her, to harness her like the wild horse she was. It was that special time of the month and her hormones were raging out of control, fantasies firing like 5.56 rounds from a big scary AR15 all through her neurons. What a rush.

She heard a knock on the door- probably a delivery of cocaine or donuts. So she simply said, in a sassy manner, "you may enter!" But it was not a donut delivery, it was Big Don- burly form barely framed in the doorway. He leered down at her, clutching a plastic bag in each hand.

"Nice decor" he said, gazing slowly around the room, decorated with art illegally imported from Africa, much of it made from poached mahogany or elephant ivory. There was even a whale bone box in one corner of the room full of ambergris that would have resulted in a twenty year prison sentence. "I like the art, looks like it's pretty new though. All my African art at the Maralago is from the colonial period. Tea tastes better when it comes from a former colonial territory, don't you know?"

"Donald... I could get in trouble. Don't tell any..." she trailed off, hoping he wouldn't disclose her whale bone box to anyone. The ambergris had a peculiar, musky scent, so she vetted her visitors well, lest some perfume aficionado get her fired.

"Ah it's all good. We love you around the maralago, seriously, stupendous propaganda, you do a good job, so I got you something." Trump dumped the bags out onto her desk. Inside were books. She picked one of them up, and read the title, then another, and another- all of the books were straight-up misogyny.

"'The humiliation of the female'? 'Tending your brap farm'? Donald, what makes you think I would read these? Get out of my office, you crazy bigot!" She screamed at him, but her throbbing pulse was sending blood somewhere other than her small, smooth brain.

"Oh Karine I know what you people are into" he replied, chuckling at one particular title; "a five thousand part guide to the female sex drive", "Now, get reading, I'll be sending you a quiz on Friday. Friday is a great day, you get to look forward to working on the weekend, or maybe golfing. I haven't decided my itinerary yet." Donald turned and left silently, the door barely clicking as he closed it with patient care. The book pile was immense- fifty titles in all. And she had to study them in only four days. It would be a long night and day, she canceled her press corps appearance, spending hours and hours titillating her foul breasts and her ovulating tunnel-bud as she studied what she *must* be, what she *must* do, for he, himself, Big Don, had commanded it. Servant-like, she wept with joy, discovering her true kink. She wanted to be commanded, and the one man in the world able to do so, had done just that. She passed out from exhaustion, waking up to find a single breakfast taco on her desk, crying loudly in joy to heaven.

DAVIE STORY

Davie was an antigun gun nut. He was also smoking meth. What a fun day.

He emerged from his parents' basement and skipped over to the little gun range they had erected so he could make his clout chasing tiktok videos. An array of weaponry sat before him; an array that would make an NRA-member, boomer fudd blush. Shotguns, revolvers, even a couple of bolt action rifles. How grand. He loaded up one of the revolvers and- in his methamphetamine addled state- considered shooting himself in the arm so he could show off what big bullets could do to the human body, but he had just enough sanity left to think otherwise. He had some crack too, and smoked it. When mixed with the meth it was an awfully good rush. He barely ate due to his drug addictions, and most of his calories came from drinking piss beer, so his frail, prematurely aging body was barely able to heft the revolver up and fire a couple of rounds, fantasizing about killing minorities. He was secretly racist, just like he secretly loved the rush that came when he killed a couple birds or a raccoon. He loved to watch the injured animals suffer, as all liberals secretly do, fantasizing when they bite into a nice porterhouse steak.

But there was something in the treeline which caught his attention. It wasn't a deer- and anyways he didn't have anything large enough to take one down. It wasn't a bear, although fatty bear meat sounded awfully good. It was a man. And that man was grinning, about thirty yards distant, but rapidly closing that gap, half-jogging towards him with a few security officers pacing behind. It was Donald Trump himself.

Trump jogged up the shitty, prefab railing of his families' deck, where Davie stood, dropping the gun down because the weight of a revolver was too heavy for his anemic arms. Then he straightened up, slightly out of breath, grinning, and holding a massive weapon that looked more like something from a Vietnam War flick than anything a civilian should own.

"Hey Davie!" He jovially shouted, "Here's a gift! Straight from the US surplus. We had surplus oil when I was president, all topped off, now our oil supply is bullcrap." He handed the gun to Davie, who struggled to even lift the thing. "Here, take some ammo. This'll be unbelievable."

The rifle was clearly in a heavy caliber although Davie did not know what caliber it was. He was more used to shotguns or a little .22- what he didn't know was that it was actually a .50 cal. The rounds dwarfed anything he had seen and looked like miniature missiles. This disconcerted him, even through his haze of meth and crack.

"Ok Davie it's time to shine you gun expert you. Pick me off that goose over there by the field. We'll be eating high on the hog today, well, high on the bird. I know you're high too. You should quit that stuff. I never even smoked a cigarette."

Trump got in beside him and Davie took a shot. The goose was practically vaporized- something he normally ascribed to the AR15 but now he was using a truly powerful gun. The shot rocketed the gun back into his calcium deficient, pathetic shoulder, and cracked it. The pain was significant.

"Donald!" He cried out, like an apostle calling out to Jesus, "That's too much!"

"No it ain't kid! You rifleman you, under your guy you'll probably get drafted. Might as well train now. Enjoy your future career and all."

Davie, cracked-up and half mindless of the pain of his

cracked shoulder, chambered another round from the beastly weapon and, while his .22 short stiffened in his pants, unloaded another .50 cal across the field, this time managing to nab another goose. It was going to be feast time after all.

Sadly, his anemic, skeletally inferior shoulder was effectively decimated by the recoil. His shoulder blade and attendant collar bone both shattered from the hit, and he fell to the floor, in exquisite pain, thereafter passing out.

When he came to, Donald himself was preparing several geese at his families' kitchen table. Davie was in a cast and had clearly been operated on. "Don't worry Davie" said Trump as he sharpened his knives to serve the geese, "I know a little bit about surgery!" He sliced up the geese, which had been cooked with berries and herbs and all manner of good things, and were perfectly seasoned and prepared. His little .22 short fired in his pants as the feast was laid before him, his parents and other guests applauding Big Don for his culinary finesse. He had finally been shown the meaning of power. He longed to fire the big gun again. He longed for Donald to be his father. He longed and lusted for power. The seed had been sown- Davie no longer wanted edamame and soylent for breakfast. He had a hankering for about six scrambled eggs, a platter of sausages, and a tankard of beer. He wanted to be a *real* man, just like his goose-cooking hero, Donald. He considered the possibility of worshiping at the temple of iron so he would stop having brawny dudes kick sand in his face at the beach while with his girlfriend- who he totally didn't think got with him for his modest e-fame and potential income.

"Careful Davie" said Trump, as he gazed down at the bird he was carving into slices, "with power comes responsibility... lose the tankard."

MITT STORY

Mitt spent his morning as he usually did; he wasn't allowed to drink coffee but there was a tea workaround in his religion; after all, black tea had some caffeine in it. So he sucked down two cups back to back, still in his comfy fuzzy robe and bunny slippers, smashing a donut into his mouth and a carrot into his asshole at the same time. It was sublime. A carrot enema was just what he needed. He took a crap at the edge of his car garage, knowing the "help" would clean it up long before he got home. What a fun morning. He briefly pretended to read a newspaper and do other "normal" morning things but his mechanical mannerisms belied his being distracted by thinking of famine children. He chuckled.

Just then he heard a strange noise. Someone was in the shower. "That's odd" he muttered to himself. He would never allow his non-white servants to use his shower, because he did not want to catch cooties. His wife was out banging the buck at his property, so it wasn't her. Nobody else, that he knew of, was even in his home. He could call the cops but they might find his stash of cocaine and tell the Mormon authorities- so that wouldn't do. And he didn't own a gun aside from a single action shotgun his grand-dad gave him, because weapons made after the early 20th century were scary and should be banned.

He grabbed up the crab hammer in his kitchen, and took off his bunny slippers, and investigated. It was the lower floor bathroom where the shower noise emanated from- not one of the seven bathrooms upstairs, nor the one in his car elevator which he installed so he could clean off the scent of poor people whenever he had to go out in public. The door was ajar, and inside he could hear someone muttering to themselves about building walls and taco bowls. He had a sneaking suspicion he knew who it was, and such a powerful, big man is not to be disturbed, so he waited outside the bathroom, getting ASMR tingles from the humming and mumbling, as the man himself (as Mitt supposed it was) continued to bathe, or do whatever he was doing. Although he was mortified by the intrusion, he was also enticed badly, and squeezed his elderly legs together, a small trickle off pee coming out of his willy, like a girl at a Beatles concert in 1964, losing control of their urinary function.

The shower stopped. Trump- as Mitt deduced he was- was there, and stood drying himself off with Mitts towels. Then he cleared his throat meaningfully about five times, and proceeded to dress. He never came to the door- oh what sadness!- but Mitt could hear him breathing on the other side as he shuffled clothing around.

"Sorry Mitt, had no choice. Just went to a huge, beautiful rally, kind of like the ones you'd have if anyone supported you. Anyways a crazy Democrat rushed the stage and tossed a bunch of piss on me. I think it was animal piss. I hope it wasn't Democrat piss, I might get AIDS. I rented a room to Freddy Mercury once. He died of AIDS. Sad, talented guy. Really liked David Bowie too, met him a couple times. Good music, weird eyes. I sold him a house, too, Mitt."

Trump breathed heavily for a minute, then walked, apparently, to the window, hefting himself outside, and it opened with a creak. But while Mitt waited, stood there, waiting to lick the floor of the shower, Donald gave him one last surprise. "Oh Mitt I think I fucked up your drain. Sorry. I have beautiful hair, but everyone loses hair sometimes. You have really short hair. I comb mine over. It's called 'the look'- some of us have it, some don't. Think that was a song by Prince once, you got the look, or something like that. The eighties were great. No antifa. Just gimme a minute and I'll be outta here. Gotta go to another rally. America waits for no man."

Trump chuckled repeatedly as he exited the window of Mitts' bathroom, then all was silent after the noise of the window closing again. Mitt could barely wait. He entered like a madman, slipping on the slick floor and managing not to crack his skull. "At least I'm not like Biden" he said, struggling across the floor like an elderly baby on his hands and knees, jubilant as a kid at Christmas day.

The drain indeed had some hair in it. Mitt writhed along the wet floor like a snake towards the drain, moaning and dragging his peepee along through water which contained the holy atoms of Donald himself. He reached out, and grasped the small clump of blonde hair in the drain, mixed with some stray grays. He marveled at the gift.

And then he slowly proceeded to eat it.

Yes, he chewed Donald Trumps hair straight from the drain, still warm, with the vague overtone of shampoo (an expensive one, of course) which Big Don had borrowed for his after-rally bathing needs. It was sublime. He chewed and chewed, working little bits of drain hair into his teeth and flossing bits of donut out- Trump was obviously a master dentist, as he had mastered everything else, Mitt mused to himself. He swallowed precious strands of the hair, and saved just a few for display. He knew his wife would get all hot and bothered just being in the same room with them- after all, she nearly fainted when he became a senator and was rubbing elbows with such a stud. He managed to orgasm, lying on the floor in a puddle of semen, water, and loose hair, exhausted and fulfilled. The day had begun in sheer jubilation.

MAXINE STORY

Maxine was suffering deeply- her cracked, wrinkled skin was folded over like the creases in a letter delivered by the US postal service, and no amount of lotion seemed to suffice to ameliorate her skin condition. She shouted to her personal staffer to bring her more lotion, which was speedily accomplished, but it was all in vain. Her neck sag and jowls wubbered around like she was a fucking turkey, causing the staffer to quietly, silently, beat a hasty retreat.

"Being old is bullshit" she muttered as she smeared lotion on her long-unused privy parts, "you don't get wiser, you just fall apart."

Just then, a stretch limo flanked by two patrol cars pulled up in the little roundabout in front of her home. Swaggering out of the limousine was none other than the man himself... Big Don. He was carrying some sort of hefty load in each hand, and as he approached closer, she could see they were milk pails. Indignant at the approach of the orange oaf, she smeared one last splattering of lotion on her face, making her look like a reverse minstrel, as she hopped on board the elderly stair lift and scooted her ass downstairs.

She got to the door before him, prepared to launch into a fiery tirade about not allowing bigots to sit down and eat at restaurants or pump gas at the gas station (after all, gasoline contributing to the climate crisis) but Trump had clearly jogged the last few steps and shoved his way inside, laughing and nearly knocking her over, hefting the pails up onto the entryway table and staring at her like a statue.

"Well Maxine I got what you need. I knew you needed some of this stuff. Think they use it in Uruguay. Beautiful country, not much investment opportunity. Lots of beef production. We have to outcompete the Chinese or we will lose millions of jobs."

He gestured to the buckets. They were filled with some sort of slimy, off-white substance. "This is Uruguayan cattle semen" he explained, "best lubricant in the world. I never need lubricants on my skin, My skin is perfect. It's America-flesh." He continued to gaze, as Maxine grabbed her prize- in a single motion, she dumped the bull sperm all over herself, not even waiting for Trump to continue speaking, soaking her body and her clothes, enraptured. It had been a while since she had encountered sperm of any kind. "It costs about fifty bucks for a shot" Trump continued, as she moaned and soaked herself with the second bucket. "I know you're a rich, nasty lady, but I need something in return. The sperm will smooth your skin, you'll be smoother than Don Juan at a strip club. Here." He had one of his aides bring in a machine. "This is a breast pump. Here's the deal. I make your skin problem go away, and you provide some breast milk for a few scientific experiments. I'm trying to cure cancer. Joe failed. I won't." He hatched the breast pump into an electric outlet along the wall and Maxine obeyed like a waif- hooking it up to her pendulous, drooping breasts, and titillating herself. "Alright" Trump said simply, "I expect both pails to be full in a fortnight. Make sure to refrigerate them. Oh, here's some estrogen shots. Got them at the local gay bar. Friendly people. Everyone seemed to want to pet my hair. Unbelievable."

Trump left a ponderous tray of needles on the table and departed as quickly as he had arrived, Maxine pumping her elderly boobs and injecting estrogen like a heroin junkie. In a few days, she felt lively, strong, lithe, she was pumping those miserable milk sacks like a drunken racecar driver pumps the gas pedal. When the buckets were full, she, human cow that she was, left them in a cooler on her doorstep. The following day, a single note appeared in familiar script. "Thanks, on behalf of the suffering cancer kids, I passed the right to try act. Yuge." It read.

RONNIE STORY REDUX

It was 10PM... it was time.

Little Ronnie had been locked away in the nut ward for months. He passed the days doing depraved things like smearing poo and drinking his own urine, and for a while it was grand- Big Don had granted him the limitless freedom of being able to wander around his padded room naked and insane, one eye slightly cocked to the side after he needed surgery to more or less correct it. After all, he had pulled it out of the socket to impress Donald, and thought he had been quite successful.

Long nights were spent pacing through his own slurry of urine and feces, interrupted by brief slumbers which brought fitful dreams in which the big man was once again telepathically summoning him.

So he needed to break out.

The plan he hatched was flawless. He began bottling his own pee and poo and hiding the bottles in an unused storage closet nearby. He had spent a week pretending to be sane, and with difficulty, managed to gain hall privileges, although he had to choke back laughter on a constant basis as he delusionally fantasized about vaulting over the counter in the cafeteria in order to urinate all over the food. After that week, he had a nice jar of fermenting feces, and he knew the scent of that stuff would knock a person out.

So at 10PM when the nightly did a pre-bedtime check to make sure he was being a good boy, he fondled the jar under the bed lovingly, as though it were his human child. He called the night nurse in, complaining of chest pain.

When the orderly turned to go fetch the on-site physician, Ronnie leaped out of his bed, completely naked, his wang stiff as a flagpole as his excitement peaked- he swung the jar and hurled a wave of fermenting piss and shit into the poor mans' face- blinded by the ammonia and gasping and vomiting, he reeled back and fell right over a small table which stood by the door- which had been given back to Ronnie for good behavior. Ronnie had loosened one of the legs of the thing and grabbed it as he bolted out the door before the excrement smell could make him pass out. Straight past the security desk in front he jogged, slamming the table leg into the head of the officer as he moved by, sending the man toppling from his chair, knocked out completely. Then, he managed to exit the psych ward- after all, like all government and quasi-government locales, security was lax- the password on the exit door was "1234."

Donald was having an event, he knew, not that far away-he had come to rail against China mostly, as the city had seen its industry gutted by foreign competitors. So he raced down the street, naked and insane, and hurled the half empty shit jar through the windshield of the first gas guzzling SUV he saw.

"Dumb muthafucka!" He shouted, laughing with delight as his rampage continued, smashing mailboxes and car windows as he ran down the street, pooping himself while running, effortlessly. Passing a few street hookers, he took a piss while still moving, his half-erect wang not impressing them in the least.

Ronnie was on the warpath.

The speaking venue was close- in a field were assembled a few thousand people, listening to Trump just about wrapping up his remarks. He could see the big orange goofball on the stage, still telepathically speaking to him. Ronnie was glad that the dinner that night had been chili con carne and had not only managed to obtain seconds, but had downed half a bottle of

Tabasco sauce with it. He needed extra bowel power if he was going to impress such a powerful man. He charged through the edge of the crowd, and because he was coated in a slick layer of shit, people got out of the way instead of attempting to stop him. Trump noticed the commotion.

"Oh look, it's an old friend. I see your beauty regimen hasn't changed..."

Ronnie stood defiantly, pausing before the stage, there in a field which had already been full of cow manure. He squatted down, and let loose- a torrent of fetid liquid poured from his ass as he urinated the last drops he still had in his bladder, then stood up pridefully as though he was accepting some sort of award.

"Yo, Donnie shitface!" he thundered. "I just made a running mate for you! You dumb fucker!"

Trump stood in silence. The crowd was disgusted and some of the people in it wretched and puked. This in turn caused other people to puke. Ronnie stood, clapping his hands and beaming as he caused hundreds of people to uncontrollably regurgitate. The ground was slick with everyones' dinner. Surely, Big Don would reward him.

But his reward never came. Two nut ward attendants in the crowd recognized him and seized his arms, hauling him to the on-site ambulance to get strapped in and sent back to the loony bin. Trump waved as Ronnie was dragged away, ranting in delusion about his power. Donald placed a simple call to the staff there, telling them Ronnie should probably not be given good behavior privileges again for a while.

THE END

Printed in Great Britain
by Amazon